N
VAN

GW00501890

love:
a field guide
for **single**
adults

little
book
series

First published in 2008
Copyright © 2008
Reprinted 2011

All rights reserved. No part of this publication may be
reproduced in any form without prior permission from
the publisher.

British Library Cataloguing in Publication Data.

A catalogue record for this book is available from the
British Library.

ISBN: 978-1-906381-09-7

Published by Autumn House Limited,
Grantham, Lincolnshire.

Printed in Thailand.

All texts are taken from the *New Living Translation*
unless indication is given to the contrary.

Other versions used:
GNB = *Good News Bible*
J. B. Phillips New Testament in Modern English
NASB = *New American Standard Bible*

There are four things that are too
mysterious for me to understand:
An eagle flying in the sky,
A snake moving on a rock,
A ship finding its way over the sea,
And a man and a woman falling in love.
Proverbs 30:18, 19, GNB

Most of us have had very little instruction in how to choose a mate, and yet we are expected to make a brilliant choice.

Statistics indicate how often we are wrong.

We desperately need to re-evaluate mate-selection procedures!

This book will help you –

- Stop drifting and take charge of your relationship

- Educate yourself about what you want and need from the opposite sex

- Avoid relationships with emotionally unhealthy persons

- End dead-end relationships forever.

Many people spend less time seriously considering what they want from a relationship than they spend on what clothes they will wear to work the next day. If you want to find someone to love you, with whom you can have a satisfying, nourishing relationship, you must have a plan of action.

Those who count on luck and chance, passion and romance alone are those who are going to end up with disappointing marriages.

The principles in this book comprise recent scientific research and durable biblical teaching. When you combine these two sources of wisdom, you will have a significantly better chance of making wise decisions about the person you marry.

The choice of a marriage partner is one of the most important decisions you'll ever make. If you choose wisely, your life will be satisfying and fulfilling. If you make a serious mistake and your marriage fails, it will cause you and your children, and all the generations to follow, immeasurable pain.

The best way to prevent getting involved in an unhealthy relationship and the tragedy that follows is to slow down.

Slowing down romantic relationships allows time carefully to analyse your emotional health and the emotional readiness of your dating partner and provides the opportunity for hidden difficulties to appear.

"'For I know the plans I have for you," says the Lord. "They are plans for good and not for disaster, to give you a future and a hope. In those days when you pray, I will listen. If you look for me wholeheartedly, you will find me."'
Jeremiah 29:11-13

*'I made a covenant
with my eyes not to
look with lust at a
young woman.'*
Job 31:1

To establish an emotionally healthy
relationship, a person needs a positive
self-image. Unless you like yourself, you
are neither capable of making intelligent
decisions about love nor ready to form
a romantic relationship with another person.

No relationship can be healthier than the two persons involved. A critical question for two people to answer before considering a lifelong partnership is: How solid is our individual self-worth?

'How can a young person stay pure?
By obeying your word.
I have tried hard to find you –
Don't let me wander from your command.
I have hidden your word in my heart,
That I might not sin against you.'
Psalm 119:9-11

Every time you compare yourself to
someone else, you will come out second
best. When you *feel* second best, you will
act second best.

The greatest barriers to successful romance are feelings of worthlessness, inadequacy and failure.

The first relationship in which you must achieve success is a love relationship with yourself. You must first feel that you are worthy and lovable.

'I will be careful to live a blameless life –
when will you come to help me?
I will lead a life of integrity in my own home.
I will refuse to look at
Anything vile and vulgar.'
Psalm 101:2, 3

When you enter the dating arena, carefully evaluate each dating partner. Look beneath surface issues. Rush into nothing. Take your time and wait for hidden difficulties to erupt.

We tend to respond and react to others on the basis of unresolved issues and conflicts from the past.

Forgiveness is the key that sets you free – forgiveness of self and others. Forgive to the point where you will no longer allow what formerly happened to torment you.

Our own needs and problems seem less overwhelming when we help others with their problems. There is less time to wallow in self-pity when actively seeking a solution to someone else's problems. For everyone who feels rejected, unloved, and unworthy, there is someone else who is worse off.

If you have negative attitudes about yourself – resentment because of your appearance, your lack of talent, your singleness, or anything else, ask God to forgive you.

Ask God to forgive any bitterness you have had towards his creation – *you*.

Your self-worth should not be programmed
by others but rooted and grounded in the
value God places on you.

If you take God at his word, believing that
you are loved and worthwhile, then you have
a solid base from which to operate.

You will have a firm centre to your life.

'Do not let any part of your body become an instrument of evil to serve sin. Instead, give yourselves completely to God, for you were dead, and now you have new life. So use your whole body as an instrument to do what is right for the glory of God. Sin is no longer your master.'
Romans 6:13, 14

Gone are the days of strict rules of etiquette when men knew how to act and women react. Rules for the dating game have changed dramatically in the last few years and it certainly doesn't work as smoothly as is often portrayed in the movies.

The tendency is to rush into marriage
without first establishing a stable base
for a relationship.

Strong, lasting relationships must be paced
over a long period of time where 'getting to
know you' is the major theme.

For successful dating –
● Slow down
● Take your time
● Look carefully before you leap.

Stage one of a dating relationship is friendship

Get to know each other while participating in a non-romantic way in social, recreational, spiritual and intellectual activities.

Slow down the process of relationship-building and develop a strong friendship before romance is even considered.

Strong dating relationships spring from strong friendships. The more you know about developing friendships, the better you will be at the dating game.

Stage two of dating relationships: casual dating

Two friends who have been part of the same group begin to emerge as a couple.

Stage three of dating relationships: special dating

There is a growing emotional attachment between the two but they have not yet moved to real commitment.

Stage four
of dating
relationships:
steady dating

The communication skills of your partner
can and should be carefully evaluated.
Does he hear what you are saying or
does he only listen? Is he able to hear the
feelings behind your words? Does he pout
or use the silent treatment? Can hurt feelings
be addressed openly or are they stuffed and
avoided? How is anger handled and conflicts
resolved?

Stage five of dating relationships: pre-engagement

A couple's ability to communicate is the single most important contributor to a stable and satisfying marriage.

It should be worked on in this stage.

Stage six of dating relationships: formal engagement

The most important task to be accomplished during engagement is not the planning of a wedding, but having premarital counselling with a qualified pastor or professional counsellor.

Stage seven of dating relationships: marriage

Marriage should be a continuation of the romantic phase of the courtship process characterised by affection, attention, respect, courtesy and fun together.

Liking each other and being friends goes a long way in contributing to happiness in marriage. All the romantic stuff does not necessarily produce lasting love if an enduring friendship has not first been established.

The two-year rule

Marrying in haste, without taking sufficient time to check a person out, is jumping into a relationship based on assumptions. Assumptions make appalling marriage partners. Every couple, regardless of their ages, circumstances or experience, need to take two full years to evaluate their readiness for marriage.

The most important advice that can be given is: TAKE YOUR TIME.

Pacing relationships can be tough. First of all there is a strong possibility that the couple will not slow the pace sufficiently to develop the skills necessary to maintain a long-term relationship.

The second problem in rushing the stages is that there is insufficient time for infatuation, romantic glow, or existing 'masks' to slip and reality to set in.

Because of the intense attraction between the sexes, it seems more exciting to be 'in love' and all that goes with it than to exercise self-discipline, slow things down, think things through and pace the relationship properly.

Some activities build relationships slowly at the friendship level; others rapidly hurl couples towards physical intimacy.

Better go for the participation date, during which you are actively involved in recreation.

Initiate contact

If you sit around waiting for others to initiate
contact with you, you will have very few
dates, but if you risk falling on your face,
you may find the love of your life.

Being selective

It is only natural to desire attractive and popular people to date. But many men or women make great dates even though they wear glasses, are short, overweight, quiet, or are not beauty contest material.

Sometimes the best 'finds' haven't blossomed yet. Avoid being shallow and looking only for physical beauty. Some interesting people come in plain packaging.

Learn techniques for being a good conversationalist *and* a good listener.

A good conversationalist can almost talk her way right into the heart of another person.

Being single does not
make you abnormal.
The Great Healer
can take your painful
loneliness and turn
it into an enjoyable,
fruitful and productive
experience if you
will allow him.

Dealing
with conflict

Any couple who wants a harmonious
relationship and a lasting marriage is
going to have to learn how to manage
conflict constructively.

The ability of a couple to manage conflict
is more important than how much in love
they are, how compatible they are, or any
other factor.

It is very important to discuss and understand each other's current and long-term goals and values. Some couples attempt to set aside conflicting ideals saying that it doesn't matter, it will work out in time, but different goals and values can drive a couple apart.

*'Don't team up with those who are
unbelievers. How can righteousness
be a partner with wickedness? How can
light live with darkness? What harmony
can there be between Christ and the devil?
How can a believer be a partner with
an unbeliever?'*
2 Corinthians 6:14, 15

Put-downs

Red flags should go up any time you are put down. If your date makes remarks about how stupid or clumsy you are, if he criticises the way you dress or behave, you can be sure that more criticism will follow. Healthy relationships affirm your worth and make you feel better about yourself.

Make it clear early in a relationship that you will not tolerate put-downs or negative remarks. If your partner refuses to stop, get out of the relationship before your self-worth is destroyed.

'Do not team up with those who are unbelievers. . . .'

2 Corinthians 6:14, 15

There are scores of Christlike men and women in our churches who are married to unbelievers. But they all carry the pain of spiritual loneliness. God gave us this command to help us avoid such pain.

You can't build a house from two separate blueprints.

One reason spiritual compatibility is so important is that during a time of stress, both can tap into a source of strength to carry them through adversity. No couple goes through life without being touched by adversity or tragedy. This imperfect world carries much evil, heartache, pain, disappointment, illness, emotional upheavals, financial setbacks and death. What a difference it makes in a marriage when both partners can turn to God in the midst of turmoil.

Relationships on a BTN basis (better than nothing) are unsound.

If you are in a relationship that does not help you feel good about yourself, but instead eats away at your feelings of self-worth, it becomes critical to end it.

How you cope with broken romance when it happens tells a lot about you. There are dignified ways to survive. If you can handle a break-up with a little class, it will do wonders for your self-esteem and help you save face.

At any cost, avoid
marriage on the
rebound. These
marriages have little
chance of success
because they usually
aren't based on
long acquaintance,
matched backgrounds,
shared values and
maturity.

Remember, just because someone has broken off with you does not mean that no one in the world wants you or that you are not a worthy person. You may be tempted to bask in your own misery and pain while trying to enlist the sympathy of friends. But a better course of action is to put the past behind you and leave it there. Dwelling on the past will only lead to self-pity and depression.

Pity parties are lonely affairs.

God knows and cares about what has happened to you. Tell him how you hurt, and ask him to help you heal. Claim the promise that *'in all things God works for the good of those who love him'*.
Romans 8:28

God has a purpose in allowing hurt to touch our lives. It teaches us to respond by seeking a closer walk with him. Whatever the reason hurt enters your life, you must trust God.

Full recovery from the pain of a break-up takes time.

Psychologists have discovered that people go through fixed stages following intense grief. This process applies regardless of the kind of loss – death of a loved one, divorce, or the break-up of a serious relationship.

When you have truly loved someone, the breaking up process will be as if a part of you is being cut off. Even if you want to be rid of this person, you will still pass through this stage.

The greatest hazard in life is to risk nothing.
In risking nothing you may avoid some future
hurt, but you cannot grow, change, learn to
live, or relate better with others. No one is
chained to the heartbreak of a broken
romance.

Peace comes as you let go of the hurt and
risk loving again.

Some things remain constant, no matter how much the world changes. One of those constants is the desire to love and be loved. We all need that feeling of belonging and caring that is the result of being 'in love'. In return, there is nothing that produces more happiness and security than the assurance that someone cares deeply about you.

The need to love and
be loved is at the very
core of our being.
The search for
intimacy to fill this
need is deep-seated.
It begins when we are
born and it never ends.

What is love?

Try out these three definitions.

- Love is a state of perceptual anaesthesia.

- Love is a grave mental disease.

- Love is a fiend, a fire, a heaven, a hell, where pleasure, pain and sad repentance dwell.

How about these three definitions?

- Love is a folly of the mind, an unquenchable fire, a hunger without surfeit, a sweet delight, a pleasing madness, a labour without repose, and a repose without labour.
- Love is a feeling you feel when you feel you are going to get a feeling you never felt before.
- Love is when two people are under the influence of the most violent, most insane, most delusive, and most transient of passions, and they are required to swear that they will remain in that excited, abnormal, exhausting condition continuously until death parts them.

Love is a learned response, a pattern of actions and reactions observed in early life.

Siblings, birth order, peers and society all contribute to our lessons in learning how to love.

Love affects brain chemistry. One study concluded that once the emotional state has been defined as 'love', there is an increase in the brain chemical phenylethylamine that maintains the emotional high. Interestingly enough, that chemical compound is found in chocolate, a popular gift for those in love.

Lovers may have sweaty hands, butterflies in the stomach, dilated pupils and so on. Such physiological effects tend to fade in time. Personally, I'm glad about that. I'd be exhausted after forty years of going through all that every time Harry walked through the door!

People in the early 'in love' stages should listen to the candid observations of others precisely because it is so easy to be blinded by romance.

Outside evaluation by a party not emotionally involved is essential!

The phrase *falling in love*, implies falling into love with the heart only. But falling in love with the heart is only a portion of the love process. Falling in love will involve your head as well as your heart.

Love is complex.
It does not strike
unexpectedly, like a
star falling from the
heavens. True love
comes only when
two individuals have
reorientated their lives,
each with the other
as the new focal point.

Men rarely feel an urgency to evaluate
a woman over time when her looks are
appealing. If she sets his hormones
racing, he knows it's love. Thoughts of
her home-making abilities, how she'll look
in twelve years after three children, and
what kind of a mother she'll make all take
a back seat.

Women look at love differently from men.
Generally women take longer to decide and
are unwilling to declare undying love until
they have assessed a man's inner qualities.
They look for characteristics they desire in
the father of their children. Women, more
than men, have an ability to look into the
future and visualise what a marriage will
be like.

Romantic love is too intense to last. If a couple marries on the basis of romantic love alone, they will be unprepared to deal with the natural tapering off of romantic feelings that occur shortly after marriage.

The ideal is unselfish love, characterised by giving, forgiving and caring. It is a nurturing love that can deny self to give to the other. Such a love survives when emotional pain is created by the one loved. This love puts the needs of the other before its own. It delights more in giving than receiving.

'Don't you realise that those who do wrong will not inherit the Kingdom of God? Don't fool yourself. Those who indulge in sexual sin, . . . commit adultery, . . . or are abusive . . . – none of these will inherit the Kingdom of God.'

1 Corinthians 6:9, 10

'Run from sexual sin! No other sin so clearly affects the body as this one does. For sexual immorality is a sin against your own body. Don't you realise that your own body is the temple of the Holy Spirit, who lives in you and was given to you by God? You do not belong to yourself, for God bought you with a high price. So you must honour God with your body.'
1 Corinthians 6:18-20

Test for love. Love develops slowly; infatuation rapidly.

Love grows, and growth requires time.

Love relies on compatibility; infatuation relies more on chemistry and physical appearance.

Many who marry because of chemistry wake up later to deal with disastrous relationships. Relying on chemistry alone to guide you towards love is dangerous.

When you're in love you are interested in the way the object of your love thinks and responds to situations.

You will focus on the values you hold in common.

Love centres on
one person only;
infatuation may
involve several people.
An infatuated person
may be 'in love' with
two or more persons
at the same time!

Love produces security; infatuation produces insecurity.

Jealousy does not signify healthy emotions but insecurity and poor self-image.

Love recognises realities; infatuation ignores them.

Love motivates positive behaviour; infatuation has a destructive effect. Love will have a constructive effect on your personality and bring out the best in you. By contrast, infatuation has a destructive and disorganising effect on the personality.

Love recognises faults; infatuation ignores them.

Some people want love so badly that they live in denial, shielding themselves from fears they think they can't handle. Love recognises the good, but is not blind to problem areas in the loved one's personality.

Love controls physical contact; infatuation exploits it.

Love respects the other person so much that it voluntarily puts on hold the desire for sex.

Love is selfless; infatuation is selfish. Being in love involves more than just the emotions. Genuine love is acted out in everyday life.

The test of love is whether you can be loving when your partner has treated you unfairly, neglected your needs, forgotten your birthday, or been inconsiderate.

Love survives the test of time; infatuation can't wait.

Infatuation wants to rush the relationship. Pulsating emotions overrule good sense and people rush into commitments that may be regretted in all the years to come.

Don't make quick commitments that you'll regret later. True love can survive the test of time.

Most fail to understand that you don't 'fall' in love. You *decide* to love – to think about, spend time with, and have strong feelings for someone.

'Falling' is the easy and fun part of love. The hard part, the commitment to love unconditionally an imperfect person, follows. Genuine love says, 'I will love you unconditionally even when you fail to meet my needs, . . . behave stupidly, make choices I wouldn't make, hurt me, disagree with me. . . .'

Biblical love

In the New Testament, five Greek words are used to define love.

Epithymia – a strong physical desire that results in sex.

Eros – refers to arousing sexual desire. It can be controlled and positive, or uncontrolled and sinful.

Storge – a natural affection implying loyalty and commitment.

Phileo – a friendship love that should have high priority in a marriage.

Agape – the highest type of love; it is an act of the will, not based on feelings. It values and serves the loved one.

Agape love means wanting the best for your loved one, even if the best opposes your personal wishes. Love means encouraging and supporting each other's dreams, even if it costs you something. It means wanting your partner to achieve and become all he can be, even if it becomes threatening to you.

This kind of love is God's creative gift to us and can be enjoyed to its fullest only within the safety and security of marriage.

Love is fragile and needs constant nourishment to flourish. *Agape* love involves a God-like ability to love even when we are not loved in return. And, like God's love, it endures.

It is suggested that love in old age, no longer blind, is true love. For love's highest intensity doesn't necessarily mean its highest quality. Glamour and jealousy are gone; and the ardent caress, no longer needed, is valueless compared with the reassuring touch of a trembling hand.

A true
forever Friend

Rather than securing all your hopes and
dreams to a human being, why not secure
yourself first and foremost to someone who
will never change? Jesus is always the same
yesterday, today and forever. Any promise he
makes, he will keep. His love is unconditional.
He will always love you, regardless of your
appearance, failures or mistakes.

If a man says, 'If you love me, you'll let me,' reply, 'If you *really* love me, you won't ask.'

If a man says, 'Everybody's doing it. We're not kids any more. What's the matter with you?' in the age of AIDS reply, 'What's RIGHT with it?'

If a man says, 'Honey, we plan on getting married anyway. Our love is greater than any slip of paper,' reply, 'In case we ever changed our minds about each other, I wouldn't want you to feel obligated to me, nor do I want to have anything to regret.'

If a man says, 'What's the matter with you? Are you frigid or something?' respond, 'There's nothing the matter with me that forgetting you couldn't cure. You're history, friend.'

If a man says, 'If you don't, I'll date someone else,' reply, 'I'll pass your name around to my friends along with your threat and then I'll look for someone who will appreciate me for something beyond my body.'

If a man says, 'I won't get you pregnant. You won't catch a disease from me!' reply: 'Let's make absolutely sure that you don't have an STD or AIDS by getting tested at the nearest clinic – and then waiting six months.'

'The temptations in your life are no different from what others experience. And God is faithful. He will not allow the temptation to be more than you can stand. When you are tempted, he will show you a way out so that you can endure.'

1 Corinthians 10:13

'Let the Holy Spirit guide your lives. Then you won't be doing what your sinful nature craves. The sinful nature wants to do evil, which is just the opposite of what the Spirit wants. And the Spirit gives us desires that are the opposite of what the sinful nature desires. These two forces are constantly fighting each other, so you are not free to carry out your good intentions. . . . When you follow the desires of your sinful nature, the results are very clear: sexual immorality, impurity, lustful pleasures. . . .'

Galatians 5:16-21

'Let there be no sexual immorality, impurity or greed among you. Such sins have no place among God's people. Obscene stories, foolish talk, and coarse jokes – these are not for you. Instead, let there be thankfulness to God.'

Ephesians 5:3-5

'God's will is for you to be holy, so stay away from all sexual sin. Then each of you will control his own body and live in holiness and honour – not in lustful passion like the pagans who do not know God and his ways. . . . God has called us to live holy lives, not impure lives. Therefore, anyone who refuses to live by these rules is not disobeying human teaching but is rejecting God, who gives his Holy Spirit to you.'

1 Thessalonians 4:3-8

If a man says, 'If you don't, I'll date someone else,' reply, 'I'll pass your name around to my friends along with your threat and then I'll look for someone who will appreciate me for something beyond my body.'

Anyone, whether married or single, must bring sexual desire under God's control, minute by minute, submitting choices to him to avoid a life of heartache.

'Don't let the world around you squeeze you into its mould, but let God re-make you so that your whole attitude of mind is changed.'

Romans 12:2, J. B. Phillips' paraphrase

Our God of choice and freedom says,
'I have something for you that is better than
temporary pleasure. Follow me. Wait on me.
Deny yourselves just a small portion of the
pleasure available today and I will give
you lasting joy, peace, and a lifetime of
companionship.'

Sex outside of marriage complicates problems we already have. The answers to such problems can be found when we have a committed relationship to Christ.

Love is friendship, tenderness, self-control, selflessness, kindness, and loyalty, blended with sexual desire.

'Love seeketh not itself to please
Nor for itself hath any care,
But for another gives its ease,
And builds a heaven in hell's despair.'
William Blake on Love

*'Grief walks upon
the heels of pleasure;
Married in haste,
we repent at leisure.'*

William Congreve on Marriage

Aim high

Everyone else might say you'll never make it,
but your standards can never be too high.

It's a funny thing about life. If you refuse to
accept anything but the best, you very often
get it.

Ask God for help

An important part of your commitment
to abstinence is relying on God. Ask your
Heavenly Father for his help to remain pure.
If you and your date discuss and pray
about your commitment to abstinence, it
will produce a bond of conscience between
you and can serve as a barrier against
temptation.

Have you already gone too far?

First, admit the sinfulness of your actions.

Second, ask God for forgiveness.

Third, stop seeing each other for six months. After not seeing your partner for six months, you will be able to determine if what you have is real love or infatuation.

Choosing

Most of us think we can choose correctly at the very moment we must make the decision.

Instead, we choose according to the way we have chosen a hundred times before. Our future is not what we decide to do, but what we have done in the past. Our future actually lies behind us!

Your future will be determined by your response to choices through obedience to God. The price is high, but the rewards are limitless.

If you are mature, you will recognise that marriage is not an easy escape from reality or personal problems, but rather brings on new problems and greater responsibilities.

The inability of partners to put themselves out for the other person, to think first of the needs of their partner, accounts for much marital agony.

Aim high

Everyone else might say you'll never make it, but your standards can never be too high.

It's a funny thing about life. If you refuse to accept anything but the best, you very often get it.

The single most important goal of any couple approaching marriage for the second time should be to improve their communication skills.

Otherwise it is just another instance of the triumph of hope over experience.

We all need seriously to study Scripture relating to marriage. We need to learn what it means to have a Christ-centred marriage and how to attain it.

Never assume that because both persons are Christians or church members, they know how to make Christ the head of their home.

Family and friends often encourage a divorced person to re-enter the dating game without delay. Their thinking is that it will ease the pain. What it really does is retard personal growth.

A person simply must find out who she is as a person before again entering the dating scene.

As single-again adults re-enter the dating game, they tend to make up their own rules, feeling there are no clear-cut guidelines for adults and anything goes. A strong Bible-based moral standard is needed. Dating is a much more serious undertaking for mature adults than for teenagers. . . .

Whatever your mistakes, God will accept you where you are and set you free from the load you are carrying. God always deals with us as we are today, *now*, not yesterday or three years ago.

Today you have a fresh opportunity to approach him and go forward in faith. Paul talks about *'forgetting what lies behind and reaching forward to what lies ahead'*. Philippians 3:13, NASB

Focus your eyes, heart and mind on him. Allow him to work in your life today.

'So put to death the sinful, earthly things lurking within you. Have nothing to do with sexual immorality, impurity, lust and evil desires. . . .'

Colossians 3:5-8

Remember Joseph's response to Potiphar's wife's advances: *'How could I do such a wicked thing? It would be a great sin against God.'*

Genesis 39:9

An item in a church bulletin read: 'Spiritual growth class postponed until September.'

Spiritual growth is not something you can put off. . . .

Either we are progressing or regressing.

Remember, the world is round, and the place that seems like the end may only be the beginning.

Venture forth with new determination to rebuild your life with what you have, in keeping with God's plan.

Through Christ you can have a hope for the future that goes beyond the broken dreams, promises and hurt you may have experienced. Through Jesus you can obtain a vision of your potential if you gain the courage to face the problem – to begin to risk, to start all over again. Remodelling may require growing pains, but look to the Master Architect for the finished product.

We can learn something about devotion from cranes, those large, graceful birds with long necks.

George Archibald, a scientist, tells us about a sandhill crane that would come to the same road every night. Archibald learned from a state trooper that the crane's mate had been killed by a car at that spot. The crane would return every night and stare into the distance, waiting for her mate to come back.

Scripture tells us that God casts our sins into the depth of the ocean. Did you know that the ocean is so deep in places and the pressure so great that anything that drops to the bottom cannot be brought back to the surface? And that's exactly where God casts our sins, in a place where they can never be found again.

'We consider it essential that all persons contemplating marriage receive premarital counselling and that our young people should be instructed, beginning in adolescence, in the meaning and obligation of true Christian marriage; this instruction to be given through the Church and the home.'
Moravian Covenant for Christian Living

Prayer
for weddings

The Lord sanctify and bless you,
The Lord pour the riches of his grace
           upon you,
That you may please him,
And live together in holy love to your
           lives' end.
So be it.
John Knox

Wedding blessing

Almighty God, Giver of life and love, bless
N and N whom you have now joined in
Christian marriage. Grant them wisdom and
devotion in their life together, that each may
be to the other a strength in need, a comfort
in sorrow and a companion in joy. So unite
their wills in your will and their spirits in your
Spirit, that they may live and grow together
in love and peace all the days of their life;
through Jesus Christ our Lord, Amen.